£1

ESSEX WITCHES

"Reproduced by courtesy of the British Museum."

ESSEX WITCHES

THE WITCHES, ENCHANTMENTS,
CHARMS AND SORCERERS
OF ESSEX

by

GLYN MORGAN

SPURBOOKS LIMITED

PUBLISHED BY SPURBOOKS LIMITED
1 STATION ROAD,
BOURNE END,
BUCKS.

ISBN 0 902875 39 6

CONTENTS

SELECT BIBLIOGRAPHY

Ady, Thomas	A Candle in the Dark.
Benton, P.	A History of the Rochford Hundred.
Clarke, Charles	A Delectation of Damnable Driftes practized by Three Witches arraigned at Chelmsford in Essex, which were executed in April, 1579.
Gardner, G.B.	Witchcraft Today.
Gifford, George	A Discourse of the Subtile Practises of Devilles by Witches and Sorcerers, 1587.
Gifford, George	A Dialogue concerning Witches and Witchcraftes.
Hole, Christina	A Mirror of Witchcraft.
Hole, Christina	Witchcraft in England.
Hopkins, Mathew	The Discovery of Witches.
Hughes, Pennethorne	Witchcraft
Kors and Peters	Witchcraft in Europe, 1100-1700, A Documentary History.
Maple, Eric	The Dark World of Witches.
Mason, Mrs. C.	Essex, Its Forest Folk and Folklore.
Morrison, Arthur	Cunning Murrell.
Murray, Margaret	The Witchcult in Western Europe.
Murray, Margaret	The God of Witches.
Macfarlane, A.	Witchcraft in Tudor and Stuart England.
Notestein	A History of Witchcraft in England from 1558 to 1718
Pamphlet 1566	The Examination and Confession of Certaine Wytches, Taken at St. Oses in the Countie of Essex.
Pamphlet 1582	A True and Just Recorde of the Information, Examination and Confession of All the Witches, Taken at St. Oses in the Countie of Essex by W.W.
Pamphlet 1645	A True and Exact Relation . . .of Witches, Arraigned and Executed in the County of Essex.
Parrinder, G.	Witchcraft.
Robbins, R.H.	The Encyclopaedia of Witchcraft and Demonology.
Summers, M. (editor)	Malleus Maleficarum.
Summers, M.	Witchcraft and Black Magic.
Summers, M.	History of Witchcraft.
Summers, M.	Geography of Witchcraft.

CHAPTER I

Witchcraftes, Inchauntments, Chármes and Sorcerers

The great witch-hunts of the sixteenth and seventeenth centuries swept through Europe like a tidal wave carrying thousands of wretched suspects before it into the torture chambers. Paradoxically the ghastly tortures, the burnings and the hangings took place during the Renaissance, a period of history regarded as an age of enlightment and reason. The Church, however, shunned the light and dreaded reason. They were threats to the established order and unless checked, would erode the very foundations on which the Church was built. All those who did not believe, all who practised rites contrary to official dogma, were enemies of the Faith and had to be eliminated. Witches came within this category.

Pope Paul VIII took the first step to eradicate the canker. In 1584 he issued a Bill which made witchcraft a heresy and gave power to the Inquisitors to search out and punish all witches. The Biblical instructions were quite clear; "Thou shalt not suffer a witch to live," it said, and "A man or also a woman that hath a familiar spirit, or that is a wizard, shall surely be put to death. They shall stone them with stones; their blood shall be upon them."

The Inquisitors accepted this advice without question although they thought that the instructions were very elementary and primitive. They soon introduced refinements. Two Dominican friars, Heinrich Kramer and Jakob Springer wrote a treatise in 1486 called "Malleus Maleficarum", or "The Hammer of Witches", which was regarded as a handbook for witch hunters. Methods of detecting witches were specifically described and means of extorting a confession from unfortunate victims were narrated with relish. Johannes Junius, Burgomaster of Bamberg in Germany observed that the tortures were so horrible that even the toughest victim would confess anything, and he had ample opportunity to study the tortures since, in his Principality, the Prince-Bishop Johann von Aschhausen elicited confession by means of thumbscrew, strappado, iron boot and squassation from over three hundred citizens, then had them all burned as witches.

In England, witchcraft was not a heresy and torture was forbidden, as a general rule. Nevertheless, in Essex alone, between 1560 and 1680 about 550 people were accused of witchcraft and 74 were executed.

Was witchcraft a phenomenon unique to the sixteenth and seventeenth centuries? Margaret Meade, the anthropologist, is not alone in believing that the origins of witchcraft are to be found in the dim and distant Stone Age. She cites cave drawings of witch doctors, and reinforces her theory by noting the strong bias in present day witchcraft towards fertility ritual. As Christianity spread and as the practitioners of the Old Religion were accused of practising hellish rites, it was no longer safe for witches to express their beliefs openly. They were underground. It is therefore difficult to fathom the truth and the witches themselves have seldom been known to express openly what they really believe. Consequently, the popular idea of witches and witchcraft is much distorted. The Church, for its own reasons, did not help. Quite the contrary. It encouraged the belief that rites practised at the Sabbats were a reversal of the Christian service. They asserted that the Lord's Prayer was said backwards, the cross inverted and the wafer desecrated. The true witch, who sincerely practises the Old Religion, is offended by such a distortion of the truth. The image will persist however, because the general public wants to believe in the alleged evil practices and the press caters for their wishes. Descriptions of the sensational practices of a minority will sell more papers than a sober account of a religious ceremony.

Nobody is free from some superstition. Horoscopes are big business and Tinker Bell is very real to children. Reginald Scot, who lived in the second half of the sixteenth century lists the creatures lurking in the dark world of the unconscious — "bullbeggars, spirits, witches, elves, hags, fairies, satyrs, pans, fauns, silenes, Kit with the canstick, tritons, centaurs, dwarfs, giants, imps, calcars, conjurors, nymphs, changelings, incubus, Robin Goodfellow, the spoorn, the mare, the man in the oak, the hellwain, the firedrake, the Puckle, Tom Thumb, Hobgoblin, Tom Tumbler, Boneless and such other bugs (bogies) that we are afraid of our own shadows."

It is not surprising when medieval man felt surrounded by so many alien creatures that the idea of having a witch as a neighbour was regarded as normal. The ancient idea of what a witch should look like is not much different from the idea that exists today. She would be elderly, tall, gaunt and stooping. To Letitia Fairfield, a modern medical expert, these characteristics are typical of a person suffering from senile dementia and osteomalacia, a starvation disease. Translated into plain English, the description would tally with Scot's observation that the witches he had seen were, "lean and deformed, showing melancholy in their faces to the horror of all who see them. They are doting, scolds, mad and possessed with spirits."

Did witches actually exist or was the entire witchcraft scene a delusion? There is no simple answer. The witches of the sixteenth and seventeenth centuries fell into one of three categories. Some were born into witchcraft, some achieved witchcraft and some had witchcraft thrust upon them.

Many people firmly believed that they were witches. Their mothers and grandfathers before them had practised the craft and had passed on their knowledge, their beliefs and even their familiars. Witchcraft was their inheritance.

Others became witches by choice, believing that the unusual powers they possessed could only derive from the dark world of witchcraft. Their ability to cure illness either by administering herbal ointments and potions or simply by the hypnotic power of their personalities placed them in a class apart from the ordinary villager.

The last category was a sad and pitiful one. To it belonged those innocent people who had been denounced by their neighbours out of spite or revenge, and who had then, under torture, confessed to practices they had never heard of.

To appreciate the horror of those days it is necessary to picture an Essex dotted with small villages, lost in the deep forest or standing lonely near some desolate, windswept marsh or salting. The villagers were ignorant, uneducated and illiterate. On all sides they were beset by the hostile forces of nature. Their very existence hung on a thread. If a cow or a pig died, or the crops failed, extreme hardship and even death could follow. The lack of scientific knowledge made every failure a mystery, but an explanation for every disaster was always found, nevertheless. Scapegoats are as old as history. When that gaunt and evil-looking crone called at the cottage a few days before for a bite to eat which was refused, didn't she slouch away mumbling curses under her breath? No wonder the cow fell sick, or the crop was blighted or the baby languished! She must have been a witch after all. That little dog that skipped behind her was surely her familiar.

If somebody did not act she would go around the village bewitching anything and everything. Nobody would be safe from her evil eye. The magistrate should be informed at once. In his presence she would soon confess. Witch marks or supernumerary nipples would be found and prove that the village suspicions were right, and further simple tests would support the claim. But first all her body hair would have to be shaved off for secret charms could easily be concealed in these secret places. Then insert a long needle into her flesh. If she felt no pain or if she did not bleed, her guilt was proved.

In such an atmosphere were the Essex witch trials conducted, trials which were to disgrace the county for the next two hundred years.

CHAPTER II

First Chelmsford Trial

In 1542, Henry VIII introduced his statute against witchcraft and the persecutions commenced. The Act was repealed five years later in the reign of Edward VI but Elizabeth, after listening to a sermon delivered by the Bishop of Salisbury, it is said, reintroduced an act very similar in content to that of Henry. Although in many ways severe, the punishments were comparatively mild according to continental standards. Death was by hanging and not burning and sometimes exposure in the pillory for six hours every three months was deemed sufficient.

The first Chelmsford Trial took place three years after the passing of the Act. On the opening day the local rector, the Reverend Thomas Cole and Sir John Fortescue presided but the trial was considered of such importance that the Attorney-General, Sir Gilbert Gerard and a judge of the Queen's Bench, John Southcote, took over. The defendants were three women from Hatfield Peveril, Elizabeth Francis, Agnes Waterhouse and her daughter Joan.

On the day before the trial, Mother Francis, wife of a yeoman, confessed to her crimes. It was the age-old story of unrequited love and revenge but with the additional dimension of magic. She had seduced Andrew

Byles hoping that he would then marry her, but he refused. The rejection infuriated Francis, so with the help of her cat Sathan, she first "wasted Byles' goods" then caused his death. Next she concocted a feline recipe of wild herbs in order to abort the unwanted child of Andrew. For services rendered she gave Sathan a drop of her blood.

Elizabeth was determined to find a husband. This time the victim was Christopher Francis. Her efforts to seduce him were successful and he, when informed later that their liaison had proved fruitful, agreed to marry her. It is difficult to understand why Elizabeth wanted to marry at all. Certainly not to produce a family, for once again she sought the help of her familiar to rid her of the baby after six months; nor to live in happy wedlock, for "after they were married they lived not so quietly as she desyred, being stirried to much unquietness and moved to swearing and cursing." She was also moved to witchcraft. She commanded Sathan to lame her husband, which he did by transforming himself into a toad and jumping into one of his shoes. "And when he perceived it putting on his shoe, and had touched it with his fote, he being sodenly amazed asked of her what it was and she bad him kil it and he was forthwith taken with a lameness whereof he cannot be healed."

Elizabeth had inherited the cat from her grandmother Eve at the age of twelve. It had been with her for sixteen years, but despite this attachment, she traded it with Agnes Waterhouse, a neighbour, for a cake. Agnes felt she had a bargain when the powers of the animal were explained to her. And all the familiar wanted in return was a drop of her blood after each mission.

When the confession and further evidence was laid before the court, she was, inevitably, found guilty but despite one murder and two abortions she was sentenced to only one year's imprisonment.

Agnes Waterhouse also confessed. She was sixty-four at the time of her trial but her age did not dim her enthusiasm for her new acquisition. She decided to experiment. She commanded Sathan to kill one of her pigs. This he did and she rewarded him with a chicken and a drop of blood. No neighbour who had disagreed with her over the years escaped punishment. Some nine years before, having become tired of her husband she commanded Sathan to kill him.

Her daughter was only eighteen. She denied everything at first but on further cross-examination she admitted that on one occasion when she was alone in the house she thought she would do "as she had seen her mother doe." She called Sathan who appeared from under her mother's bed in the guise of a large dog. She wanted him to punish Agnes Brown because she had refused her a piece of bread and cheese, but he would not help her despite the offer of a red cock as a reward. His demands were Faustian — "body and soule" — nothing less, so Joan "desirious to be rydde of him, sayd she wolde."

Shortly afterwards an "evyll favoured Dogge with hornes on his head" appeared suddenly in front of Agnes Brown, scaring her so much that she was, quite literally paralysed in her right arm and leg.

Agnes was a bright girl and lost no time in informing her family and neighbours of the terrifying encounter. It was they who reported the matter to the magistrates and in due course the three witches were brought to trial.

Agnes was only twelve years old. Her evidence was accepted without question. An astonishing aspect of these trials throughout the country was the fact that children of any age could testify, even against their parents. Some modern authorities have suggested that the magistrates believed in the Biblical tenet concerning wisdom issuing from the mouths of babes. Whatever the reason, there is no doubt that such childish evidence sent many a person to an untimely death. Later, when the Bilton Boy, the Burton Boy and others were proved to be impostors the admission of such evidence was treated with greater caution.

Back to young Agnes. She wallowed in the limelight. It must be admitted that for a girl of her age she did remarkably well. She had been churning butter one day when "a thynge lyke a black dogge with the face like an ape, a shorte taile, a chaine and a sylver whystel hanging from his neck", suddenly appeared and leapt about in a frightening manner. She conquered her fear sufficiently to ask what it wanted, which was some of the newly-made butter. She denied that there was any so the dog ran to the buttery and opened the door with the key which it had in its mouth, then returned to her saying that it had churned some butter for her.

Agnes told her parents of the unusual experience. They sought the advice of the priest who, not unnaturally, suggested instant prayer. This helped the Waterhouse family, but the dog was unaffected and returned the following day still carrying the key in its mouth.

What did affect the dog though, was the mention of the word Jesus. When Agnes invoked the holy name the animal disappeared. Its liking for butter proved stronger than its fear since it returned later carrying a piece of bread which it wanted Agnes to butter. Again, she said that there was none ready, so it slunk away.

Some days later it reappeared holding a knife in its mouth. It expressed surprise that she was still alive and suggested to Agnes that it changed this condition by a quick stab in her heart. She objected and told him sharply to drop the knife in the name of Jesus. This time the holy name did not scare him. He refused saying that "he wolde not departe from his sweet dames knyfe as yet, and then I asked hym who was his dame, and then he nodded and wagged his head to your home, Mother Waterhouse."

Agnes Waterhouse was next cross-examined. She denied that she possessed a "dagger knife" only a large knife. And her daughter denied that the familiar which frightened Agnes had the face of an ape. It was a dog's face.

The Attorney-General asked Mother Waterhouse to make the dog appear in court adding, "If you can we will shortly release you."

She replied that since her daughter Joan was the one who had released it, only she could make it return. Sir Gilbert then asked her when she had last fed her cat on her blood. She denied the accusation but when the gaoler lifted her kerchief "diverse spottes in her face and one on her nose" were revealed.

"In good faith, when did thy cat last suck thee?"

"Not this last fortnight, my lord!"

This admission was enough to damn her. The jury returned a verdict of guilty and Mr. Justice Southcote sentenced her to death. Agnes Waterhouse was hanged on 29th July, 1566.

Her daughter Joan was found not guilty.

CHAPTER III

Second Chelmsford Trial

Two of the dramatis personae of the first Chelmsford Trial, Mr. Justice Southcote of the Queen's bench and Mother Elizabeth Francis of Hatfield Peverel, reappear in this witchcraft drama, which was most unfortunate for Elizabeth. This was her third conviction for witchcraft and now the law had hardened in its attitude so much so that a person found guilty had little or no chance of escaping the hangman's noose.

Elizabeth, however, had not changed. She proved to be the same mean, spiteful, revengeful harridan. Because her neighbour Mrs. Poole had refused to give her some yeast, she had threatened her with "meanness". She then thought she would try her luck with Mrs. Osborne. According to her account, as she was approaching the latter's house "a spirit like a little rugged doggee" appeared before her. The animal, no doubt recognising a soul-mate, asked her where she was going and why. It offered to help her if she would give it a small present. All that Elizabeth had at that moment was a piece of bread which although stale proved acceptable to the shaggy dog. Hunger satisfied, it departed as suddenly as it had appeared, to carry out its mission — to give Mrs. Poole a pain in the head. Mother Francis felt that the odds were against her. She was the type of person who thought it grossly unfair that she should be the only person to be accused of witchcraft when all the other witches in the village went scot free. It was common knowledge that eight years previously Elizabeth Lloyd had poisoned John Francis, and that sometime later she had given some cake to Joan Roberts and the poor girl had died.

Warming to her subject, Mother Francis then accused Mother Osborne, sister of the late Mother Waterhouse, of possessing a mark on the tip of one of her fingers and a teat on the outside of her right leg. Surely these were proof that she was a witch.

Her revelations were of no avail. She was found guilty of bewitching Mrs. Poole and sentenced to death by hanging.

Ellen Smith was charged with bewitching a child and causing its death. She had done this because her daughter had been struck by Mother Webbe of Maldon in the course of a severe quarrel. Not unnaturally, Ellen was furious when she heard what had happened and threatened revenge. Unfortunately, it was the four-year-old daughter of Widow Webbe who received the full force of her spite. Cruelly, she struck the child in the face and it died a few days later. As it declined it had been heard shouting, "Away with the witch". The following morning the grieving mother had seen "a thing like a black dog go out at her door, and presently at the sight thereof she fell distraught of her wits."

In the tense atmosphere of the village it was never difficult to find witnesses who would testify against suspected witches. A neighbour of Ellen's had once heard her quarrelling with her father, John Chaundler, over some money left her by her mother who had been hanged as a witch five years previously. Poor John did not have a chance. From that day his health deteriorated and not long afterwards, he died.

John Eilwood, too, suffered from severe body pains after refusing to give alms to Ellen's little boy, but he did not die. Indeed he survived to give evidence at the trial which corroborated the son's statement. On the night when the pains first attacked him he was sitting in front of the fire with his neighbours when he saw a rat climb up the chimney. But a toad fell down! They caught it with tongs, placed it on the fire which then burned blue. Shortly afterwards Ellen Smith burst into his house in great pain and enquired how they all were, a strange remark since she was the one who was suffering.

Her son was recalled to the witness box. Had his statements been forced out of him or did he enjoy the spotlight — like Agnes Brown in the first Chelmsford Trial? There is no way of finding out. One thing we do know though — his evidence was damning.

When asked if his mother had any spirits he replied that she had three. "One she called her Greate Dicke, which was enclosed in a wicker bottle; then her little Dicke, in a leather bottle; the third, William, she kept in a woolpack."

The bailiff who searched her house found the bottles and the woolpack but no spirits. But this evidence was enough to prove her guilt and she was hanged.

Alice Noakes, the next woman to be accused of witchcraft came from Lamberd Ende. She was an ill-tempered mother who took too seriously the pranks of young Tom Spicer. He had pretended to run away with the gloves he had playfully snatched from her daughter. Alice was not amused and angrily, shouted, "I'll bounce him," whereupon the poor lad fell to the ground paralysed. He had to be taken home in a wheelbarrow.

Even when the gloves were returned, the spell was not removed. Thomas died eight days later.

On another occasion, Mother Noakes used her evil powers on a horse. She had just quarrelled with a ploughman, so caused the animal to fall to the ground. The employer was furious when he heard, but his anger did not frighten the witch. To show her distain of the farmer she caused the horse to die.

The third charge was that she had caused a child to be still-born. Suspecting that her husband was a having an affair with Mother Tatler, she was convinced that the child she was carrying was her husband's. Neighbours were aware of the affair and of Mother Noakes' jealousy, so when the child was born dead, it was unnecessary to look far for the explanation.

Mother Noakes was found guilty of the charges and she was sentenced to death.

When Marjory Staunton was tried before Judge Gawdy, the evidence proving that she was a practising witch was so overwhelming that the verdict of guilty was inevitable.

Thomas Prat of Broke Walden recalled the day when she had called at his house and had said that she had been accused of being a witch and had been beaten for it. When invited, she recounted the incident in more detail and one of Prat's friends recorded the information.

Despite her protestations of innocence Prat was unconvinced. On one occasion when she called at his house he had scratched her face with a needle and remarked, "What, you have no flea there?" He seemed surprised that she resented such treatment! When he fell ill the following night he knew where to lay the blame. And there was the occasion when his chickens died.

Mother Staunton appeared at his house carrying grain. He had snatched a handful from her and had thrown it to the birds. They had all died.

Unlike Judge Southcote, Judge Gawdy wanted more evidence before passing sentence. This was readily provided.

After Mother Staunton had been refused some yeast at the house of Richard Saunder of Broke Walden — what had happened? A baby in a cradle had become "vehemently sick" and when it had been picked up by the mother a reliable witness had sworn that the cradle continued to rock of its own accord. The witness to this remarkable occurrence a gentleman serving the Earl of Surrey, had thrust his dagger three or four times into the cradle but it still continued to rock.

Mrs. Petrie of Broke Walden remembered the day when she had refused to give Mother Staunton the items she had requested, and on that same day baby Petrie had fallen ill and continued so for a whole year.

John Hopwood's gelding had fallen sick and died soon after he had refused to give the witch a leather thong.

And why did the cows of John Cornell the younger, yield blood instead of milk? Because he had refused to give Mother Staunton the milk she had asked for.

Only the prayers of the Vicar of Wimbushe saved the life of his child who had been made ill by Mother Staunton's spell after he had refused her some requests.

One would have thought that the villagers would have learned to be more generous with these awful examples of witchcraft happening all around them. I suppose that even in those days they never thought "it would happen to them."

William Tower was such a person. Although he must

have known Mother Staunton quite well since she called at his home every Friday, he still refused her the gifts she requested. His one child fell sick immediately. Twenty pigs belonging to Robert Lathburn of Wimbushe fell sick after he had refused small gifts to the witch. One of his cows "cast into a narrow gripe" and despite careful nursing "she was in a few days likely to be lost in the mire."

Robert Cornell of Snerson refused to fill Mother Staunton's bottle with milk. Angrily she left her own bottle and went away with a full one. Returning three days later she asked for her own bottle back, filled with milk. Brave Mrs. Cornell refused and even shut the door in her face despite the fact that she felt she was dealing with a witch. Withdrawing from the house a short distance Mother Staunton proceeded to draw a circle with a knife and to gouge small depressions inside it. When asked what she was doing she gave the oracular reply that she was making "a shitying house for herself." Next day "Wife Cornell began to swell as though she would burst and had still not returned to normal."

What an accumulation of damning evidence! Yet Judge Gawdy, discovering a technical flaw in the evidence directed the jury to return a verdict of not guilty! The judge had noted that the names of the owners of the gelding and cow had been omitted and, in his opinion, this omission made the evidence too vague. Mother Staunton was released.

Elizabeth Francis, Ellen Smith and Alice Noakes were not so lucky. They were hanged the following day.

CHAPTER IV

St. Osyth Witch Case

On May 9th 1921, a Mr. Booker of St. Osyth found a skeleton in his garden. It was that of a woman aged between forty-five and fifty and it was evident that she had suffered from curvature of the spine. The burial was in unconsecrated ground and the skeleton lay north to south. But the most unusual feature was that the joints were all rivetted at ankles, knees, wrists and elbows — a practice sometimes adopted to prevent evil spirits from haunting.

Was the skeleton that of a witch? Some experts think that the unusual aspects of the burial substantiate the claim. Besides St. Osyth was noted for its witches.

A pamphlet published in 1582 gives a full account of the St. Osyth witches, "Information, Examination and Confession of All the Witches Taken at St. Oses." The author signed himself "W.W." but it is thought he was assisted in the compilation by one of the principal characters of the drama, no other than Mr. Darcy, an ambitious magistrate.

Ursley Kempe always went quietly about her business in the remote and quiet village of St. Osyth. It would have been difficult to believe that she would become the centre of a notorious witch hunt. The whole affair started quite innocently. Grace Thurlowe's baby fell sick and helpful Ursley, who performed a little healing on the side, called at the house and offered her services free. She took the child's hand and repeated three times, "A good childe, howe are thou laden." She refused the invitation to return later and babysit because she said the child would have recovered by then, and she would not be needed. She wasn't.

Mrs. Thurlowe worked for the lord of the manor, Mr. Darcy, and when she gave birth to another child, her employer suggested she seek the help of Mother Kempe. She refused suspecting that her would-be helper was a witch. Mother Kempe was offended. A few months later the baby fell from its cot and broke its neck. The distressed mother also became unwell with acute rheumatism. Mother Kempe offered to cure her for twelve pence to which she readily agreed. For a month she was gloriously free of all pain but when she refused to pay the money on the grounds that she had none, the pains returned. Naturally she blamed the witch and reported all the unusual happenings to Mr. Darcy. Amis Letherdall, a friend of Grace, added more fuel to the fire. Shortly after she had refused to give some scouring sand to a son of the witch, her own son fell ill "with a great swelling of its belly and other privy parts." On the advice of a wise-woman, she accused Mother Kempe of bewitching her child, a charge which she denied.

The child became worse so another wise-woman was consulted to "unwitch" the sick child, but she refused to help because she thought that her powers were too weak to remove the spell.

Darcy's interest was aroused so he sent for Mother Kempe and questioned her. At first she played the innocent denying all knowledge of witchcraft. But Darcy persisted and she then admitted that she did know something of the ancient craft. She had picked up the rudiments from a Mother Cocke some ten years previously. At that time she had suffered from a "lameness of her bones" and had sought a cure. This she had obtained from Mother Cocke. The recipe was simple but revolting — cherwell mixed with hog's dung! The mixture was to be held in the left hand and pricked three times with the point of a knife. The charm was then to be thrown on the fire and, at the same time the underside of a table had to be pricked three times with the same knife. These preliminaries completed, a drink had to be prepared, consisting of a glass of ale in which three sage leaves and three leaves of Herb John had been placed. A glass of the brew was to be taken night and morning.

No patent laws existed in those days and Ursley's delight in the efficacy of the treatment prompted her to set up on her own as a herbal witch. Her first clients were Mr. and Mrs. Page. They had been "struck lame". Witchcraft was diagnosed, the stinking remedy was prescribed and the victims walked again.

Such was the atmosphere of the time that Darcy read witchcraft into a simple village cure. Or was he out to further his own ambition? Thinking himself hot on the scent of extensive witchcraft practice and realising that before him was a malleable witness, he offered her clemency if she would reveal more of her black skills. Ursley agreed to cooperate. Yes, she had four familiars named Tyffin and Jack, Pigine and Tyttey and she had trained them to specialise — a novel twist! The first pair were ruthless, they punished and killed, but the female pair caused minor inflictions such as lameness and lesser body ailments. Tyttey had punished Grace Thurlowe, and Pigine it was who had caused the "great swelling in the bottom of (the) belley and other privy parts" of the Letherdall child: And it was the "hee" Tyffin who had upset the cradle and killed the Thurlowe baby.

Darcy was delighted with the success of his mean ruse. He enjoyed his supper and continued the cross-examination later that evening. Grace Thurlowe and Amis Letherdall with her daughter confronted the alleged witch. There was no doubt that the child was ill and "the privie and hinde parts thereof were in a most strange and wonderfull case." The mother recalled that the child had called out when passing Ursley's house and actually pointed window-wards crying, "Wo, wo, wo". And it was only nine months old!

Poor, illiterate, frightened Ursley fell on her knees in front of Darcy and craved forgiveness — but to no avail. Prison for the night and further examination next morning was her reward.

Still believing that Darcy meant what he said about clemency she now offered to tell all she knew about the local witches. Darcy's promise was prompt but she was not to know that he was in no position to be clement.

Her friend Ales Newman was the first to be denounced. She had helped Ursley practise her magic and as a peace offering after a quarrel had accepted her "spirits" with a proviso that she would loan them to Ursley whenever she wanted to punish a neighbour who had offended her.

Elizabeth Bennet was also a witch. One day Ursley called on her and receiving no answer to her knocking, glanced through the window and saw a familiar like a ferret lift up a cloth and peer into the pot. She consulted Tyffin which, like some Greek oracle, announced that Ales had two "spirits", a black dog called Suckyn and

frequently combined to uncover witches; and that strain between neighbours could be a prime cause of the accusation.

He was no sceptic, however, unlike Reginald Scot, who, prompted by the St. Osyth trial, wrote "Discoverie of Witchcraft" in 1584, a book which expressed views counter to the general opinions of the day. He regarded the whole witch cult as a delusion, and held the Inquisition responsible for the growth and spread of the beliefs and for the savagery of the persecutions.

The third Chelmsford Trial took place in 1589, on July 3rd, before Robert Clarke, Baron of the Exchequer, and John Puckering, Queen's Sergeant, at a time when these conflicting views on the nature of witchcraft had to some extent reduced the temperature felt by people towards the old cult.

To read the lists of suspected witches in the Assize File is to realise that witchcraft was regarded as a crime no different from other felonies. Bold statements that so and so was accused of witchcraft are interlarded with cases of assault, robbery, etc. It is this cold accountancy, which, more than anything, drives home to us that witchcraft was regarded not as something exceptional, but as a normal part of living.

Richard Dunne and his unmarried sister Agnes, lived together in Waltham Cross. They were declared not guilty on the three counts of which they were charged. The gelding worth 40 shillings was not bewitched by them, nor were the "languishings" of Henry Ladd and Simon Beck a result of their spells.

Ellen Bett, the wife of John Bett was found to have bewitched the women in "Much Waltham" where they all lived, so that they died. The unfortunate victims were Margery Baulderson and Anne Mauning.

John Givian of Stixted lost the sight of one eye. Margaret Cony was held responsible and found guilty. She was also found guilty with Avice Cony of using "Witchcrafts, enchauntements, charmes and sorceries" to render Jeremy Browne lame in his left leg. Avice was also held responsible for causing the death of Richard Franck by witchcraft.

Both Alice Foster and Joan Harwood of Dagenham were the victims of the witchcraft of Joan Uptney, from which they died. A verdict of guilty was returned.

Alice Odell immediately "languished" as a result of the bewitching by John Dering who lived in Theydon Garnon. To add a touch of variety to the proceedings he was also found guilty of bewitching "payles of milke" belonging to Stephen Clarke, so that his servants "by no art or labour were able to make cheese thereof."

The testimonies of Joan Prentice and John Cunny were quite different from those of the other prisoners. To Joan Prentice a ferret appeared one day and claimed to be the Devil in disguise. He wanted her to sell her soul to him and she would be rewarded. At first, she refused saying it was not hers to give but the Devil would not take no for an answer and, eventually, Joan struck a bargain. He agreed to do her bidding provided she looked after his welfare and, from time to time gave a drop of her life's blood. The arrangement seemed to work. The imp, Bidd, flourished, but created havoc in the neighbourhood by his pranks.

The case of Joan Cunny was sad. Her two daughters had no moral scruples. They both had illegitimate children and had no qualms about giving evidence against their eighty-year-old mother. The aged crone was accused of kneeling in a circle she had drawn on the ground and praying to the Devil. Two imps appeared in the shape of frogs and enjoying the homely names of Jack and Jill. To these she readily sold her soul. They did her bidding, adding to the confusion of the village.

If the accused had been tried by the Inquisition not one would have escaped the death penalty. Joan Prentice and Joan Cunny were hanged. Alice Cunny was found guilty of murder but escaped hanging because she was pregnant. Margaret Cunny was remanded for a year and pilloried. The others escaped the death penalty.

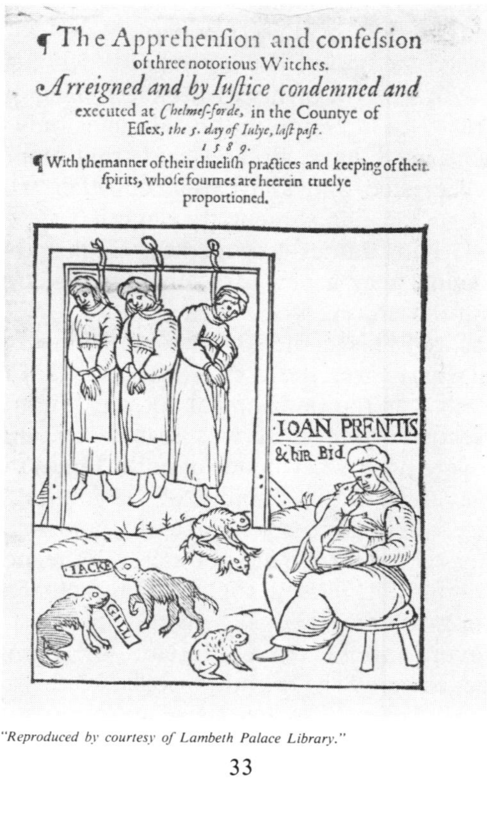

"Reproduced by courtesy of Lambeth Palace Library."

CHAPTER VI

Every Shadow an Apparition

King James VI of Scotland was so opposed to the views expressed in Scot's "Discoverie of Witches" that he commanded the book to be burned. In 1597 he counter-blasted with a book of his own called "Demonologie". He wrote: "My intention in this labour is only to prove two things, as I have already said: that such devilish arts have existed and still exist, the other what exact trial and severe punishment they merit."

In 1603 King James ascended the English throne and the following year a new Act aimed at witchcraft was placed on the Statute Book. It was more severe than its predecessors. This came as no surprise since Scottish practice was nearer the continental model. From that date, death was the punishment for any witch committing a second offence. It was stated too, that "devil marks" were positive evidence of guilt. James was also a firm believer in the infallibility of "swimming".

Strangely enough, the presence of a confirmed enemy of witches on the throne did not increase the momentum of the witch hunt. Indeed, there was an actual lull in the persecution after 1603.

However, above this plateau of comparative tolerance towered a frightful peak in the shape of Mathew Hopkins. Most people seem to have heard the name, possibly because he was portrayed by the actor Vincent Price in a somewhat bloodthirsty film.

Until the year 1644 he was an unknown lawyer with a practice in Manningtree in north Essex. Then in March of that year, as he narrates in his "Discovery of Witches", he discovered that there were "some seven or eight of that horrible sect of witches living . . . in Manningtree, with divers other adjacent witches of other towns, who every six weeks in the night (being always on the Friday night) had their meetings close to his house, and had their several solemn sacrifices there offered to the Devil."

The eight witches of Manningtree were arrested, tried, condemned to death and hanged. Elizabeth Clarke confessed after being kept awake for three days and nights. She said that the Devil who had visited her was a "proper gentleman with a laced band". She had a veritable menagerie of imps, a white cat called Holt, a black rabbit called Sack and Sugar, a greyhound called Vinegar Tom and a sandy spaniel who answered to the name Jarmara.

Elizabeth had commanded her imps to wait for a Mr. Edwardes at a bridge on the River Stour which he would be crossing when returning to Manningtree after a visit to East Bergholt. The idea was to scare the horse so that the rider would be unseated and killed. The imps could not have been at their best that day for Mr. Edwardes survived to give evidence at the trial. He even recalled vividly the inhuman shriek of "Ah! Ah!"

The Earl of Warwick officiated at the Chelmsford Assizes on July 29th 1645. He had prepared himself for the ordeal by listening to a Puritan sermon immediately before the trial. The effect on his state of mind was such that he condemned to death nineteen of the twenty-nine women arrested.

Rebecca Jones was a servant girl in Clacton, working in the house of John Bishop. The first meeting with the Devil was pleasant since he appeared in the guise of "a handsome young man". Courteously, he enquired of her health and, being assured that it was good he requested that she give him two drops of her blood. She obliged.

Her next encounter was rather frightening; on this occasion she was returning to St. Osyth when she was accosted by a man clothed in rags. He fixed his staring eyes on her, then thrust three mole-like creatures into her hands. Before she recovered from her surprise the devil commanded that she look after the imps and feed them regularly on milk. If she did this they would serve her diligently. Although they were given the homely names of Margaret, Annie and Susan they did not behave like domestic pets. One killed a sow in Clacton; another killed Thomas Bumpstead who had beaten the young son of Joyce Bone. Later, the wife of Thomas was also killed. For her sins Rebecca was found guilty and hanged.

Elizabeth Gooding was a poor, old woman. She had tried to obtain a half pound of cheese on credit from Robert Taylor, but without success. Angrily, she left the shop mumbling curses under her breath. So it came as no surprise when Taylor's horse fell sick. The skill of four knowledgeable farmers was of no avail against the witch's spell. "The belly of the horse would rumble and make a noise like a foul chimney fire."

Margaret Moore kept a veritable battery of imps, twelve in all, with diversified talents. Children and cattle could be killed, bread and beer spoiled, and as a change from the usual routine, vermin could be showered on spotlessly clean houses, as Mrs. Rawhood testified.

The sad story continued; evil gossip of spiteful neighbours, damning evidence arising from medical ignorance helped to condemn eccentric old ladies to death. Ten of the condemned were executed at Chelmsford and four burned at Manningtree. Margaret Moore died on the way to her execution. Rose Halleybread died in gaol and Rebecca West got off scot free.

One of the people present at the trial was a man called Arthur Wilson. He was the steward of the Earl of Warwick and certainly had more sense and compassion than his noble master, as the following passage from his writings indicates. He "could see nothing in the evidence which did persuade me to think them other than poor, melancholy, envious, mischievous, ill-disposed, ill-dieted, atra-bilious constitutions, whose fancies worked on gross fumes and vapours, might make the imagination ready to take any impression, and they themselves by the strength of fancy, may think they bring such things to pass which many times, unhappily they wish for and rejoice in when done, out of the malevolent humour which is in them; which passes with them as if they had really acted it. And if there be an opinion in the people that such a body is a witch, their own fears (coming when they are) resulting from such dreadful apprehensions, do make every shadow an apparition; and every rat or cat an imp or spirit, which make so many tales and stories in the world, which have no shadow of truth."

What a masterly analysis — one that a modern psychiatrist would be proud of!

Such considerations did not bother Mathew Hopkins. Indeed, spurred on by the success of his first venture into witch-hunting, he dubbed himself Witch-finder

General, recruited an enthusiastic assistant called John Stearne and a woman helper called Mary Phillips, whose job it was to search for witch marks, then travelled throughout the Eastern Counties discovering witches at twenty shillings a time. When he thought that he had unearthed a witch — he set out to make her confess — and it was a person of exceptional strength and courage who could resist the torture devised by Mathew Hopkins.

"Having taken the suspected witch, she is placed in the middle of the roome on a stool or table, cross legged or in some other uneasy posture, to which if she submits not she is then bound with cords; there she is watched and kept without meate or sleep for the space of twenty-four hours, for (they say) within that time they shall see her impe come and suck. A little hole is likewise made in the doore for the Impe to come in at; and lest it should come in some less discernible shape they that watch are taught to be ever and anon sweeping the room and if they see any spiders or flies, to kill them. And if they cannot kill them they can be sure they are imps."

In 1645 Mathew Hopkins and his assistants travelled throughout Essex, Suffolk, Norfolk and Huntingdonshire. In the first two of these counties alone, well over a hundred people were hanged, and although Hopkins did his work at the invitation of towns and villages his methods were not universally popular. John Gaule, parson of Great Staughton, not only refused to have him near the village, but wrote a damning criticism of his methods. The account of the tortures quoted above is taken from his book "Select Cases of Conscience touching Witches and Witchcraft".

The power of Hopkins was curtailed somewhat

after the Chelmsford trials since the magistrates too, disapproved of his torture methods, favouring "swimming" which had met with the approval of James I. Strangely enough, Mathew objected since it was "a trial not allowed by law or conscience" but he still used it. The victim, right thumb tied to left toe, was thrown in the water. If she sank she was declared innocent, whether she drowned or not! But if she floated she was definitely a witch.

The terrorism of the awful man was, fortunately, of short duration. He became sick and in 1647, returned to Manningtree. It is believed by many of his critics that he was hanged for witchcraft. True, he had been accused of being a witch, but he actually died in bed of consumption.

In the Parish Register of Mistley is an innocent entry:

> Mathew Hopkins, son of James Hopkins, minister of Wenham, was buried at Mistley, August 12th, 1647.

The discovery of witches and their trials did not cease with the death of the Witch-finder General, but as the second half of the seventeenth century drew to its close, attitudes were beginning to change. To the clergy belief in witchcraft was mandatory. The command, "Thou shalt not suffer a witch to live" could have but one interpretation. But these quotations from the Bible did not go unchallenged. There were men like Thomas Ady, for instance, who in his "Candle in the Darkness" asked for scriptural evidence that witches could fly and kill and could be recognised by devil's marks. It was his opinion that witches were the Popish rout. When they claimed magical powers they should be tried on that score and not for witchcraft.

Not all learned men agreed with these views. Hobbes the philosopher and Boyle, the scientist, for instance, accepted witchcraft as a part of the natural order of things although they did not clamour for dire punishment of the practitioners. This tolerance did not penetrate down to village level. Professor Trevelyan in his "English Social History" wrote: "It was lucky for the witches that England was still aristocratically governed. In many rural parts the populace, if it had not been restrained by the gentry, would have continued to drown or burn witches down to the nineteenth century."

The last official execution of a witch in England took place in Exeter in 1684. Witchcraft however did not die on that date. Four days before the seventeenth century drew to its close Widow Comon was buried on the north side of Coggeshall church. On three separate occasions she had been subjected to "swimming" by a village mob. She did not drown, but died from the effects of the cruel ordeal.

CHAPTER VII

Cunning Men

Throughout the eighteenth century the attitude towards witchcraft continued to change particularly among people of education who had access to the various books and pamphlets written to prove or disprove the age-old beliefs. An inaccessible book, however, will not have much effect on the attitude of an illiterate peasant. The observation of Lord Chief Justice Parker at a trial held in Brentwood during the summer of 1712 to the effect that if anyone died as a result of "swimming" then those responsible would be treated as murderers, had little immediate effect upon the superstitious country folk. Nor did the "Historical Essay Concerning Witchcraft" written by Francis Hutchinson and published in 1718. The arguments he marshalled to prove the cult was a delusion, that the children who were encouraged to condemn their own parents were of evil character and that many judgements of the so-called learned prosecutors were of a political nature were accepted by the educated mind but failed to penetrate to remote villages like Canewdon and St. Osyth. Nevertheless, the general climate of belief was changing from the top downwards so the repeal of the statute against witchcraft was inevitable. In 1735, the Act that had been law since the reign of James I was rescinded. But not entirely. It was still a crime to practise white witchcraft but instead of hanging, the convicted person was exposed in the pillory; this was deemed sufficient punishment.

Acts of Parliament can make certain beliefs illegal at a stroke, but they cannot change men's minds with such rapidity. The Act of 1735 simply drove the practice underground. Sudden eruptions from time to time indicated that the beliefs were still dormant.

In 1774, for example, a cruel incident took place in Rochford. John Harriott, the founder of the Thames River Police, recounts how two members of the Hart family who were suspected of bewitching cattle, were siezed by angry villagers, tied with ropes then dragged through the river behind a boat. It was indicative of the changing attitude towards witchcraft that some of the onlookers protested at this barbaric display and had the courage to rescue the unfortunate couple before they were drowned.

Such displays of primitive instinct became less frequent. Even the connotation of the word "witch" underwent a change. To call a person an "old witch" would not lead inevitably to arrest and trial. Practitioners of age-old practices were no longer called witches, the less offensive terms, wise-woman and cunning-man were used instead. These were the people now conusulted on all matters relating to healing, divination, finding lost property and removing spells from things bewitched. Their exceptional skills were admired yet feared. They were a combination of doctor, vet, fortune-teller, spell-remover, psychiatrist. Such a man was Cunning Murrell. His real name was James but the pseudonym was in the nature of a compliment to his skills. We know a great deal about him because Arthur Morrison once spent a holiday in Hadleigh and was so fascinated by the tales he heard about Murrell that he collected any scrap of information from people who had known or had heard of him. In our own days Eric Maple added considerably to this knowledge by his own diligent research.

James Murrell was born in Rochford in 1780, the seventh son of a seventh son. He was apprenticed to a surveyor in Burnham-on-Crouch before becoming a chemist's stillman in London, in which occupation he picked up a knowledge of elementary chemistry. In 1812 he returned to Essex setting up as a shoemaker in Hadleigh where he spent the rest of his life. He had twenty children so it is not surprising that his wife preceded him to the grave.

As a cobbler he was not particularly successful probably because his interests lay elsewhere. He became absorbed in ancient lore, in herbs, enchantments, astrology, and his reputation grew apace. We know from letters found in his chest and examined by Morrison that people from all walks of life sought his help in bewitching enemies, discovering treasure, curing illnesses.

He certainly knew the value of showmanship. His little cottage, which stood in Church Lane, Hadleigh, was everyone's idea of a witches parlour. From the ceiling hung herbs collected from Daw's Heath, a dark, mysterious chest squatted in the corner of the room, and on the table stood a human skull.

The client was invited into the room by Murrell, who was a small man with penetrating blue eyes, then asked the purpose of the visit. Was high or low treatment required — spiritual or material help? If the former, then "good angels" were raised to assist the wise-man. Lost property was found by gazing into a bucket containing water, on which floated a black shiny substance. If the property had been stolen the thief would be revealed if the victim stared into a mirror.

Charges were proportionate to the skill required. For witchcraft, diabolical possession or finding lost property, the fee was one shilling. For summoning forces from another world the fee was half-a-crown.

It is always difficult to distinguish between what was genuine and what was showmanship in the practices of Cunning Murrell. One remedy was rather frightening — as it was meant to be! A local blacksmith had made Murrell a quantity of iron bottles. They were used for breaking spells. A repellent mixture of urine, nail-clippings, pins, blood and herbs was sealed in the bottle which was then placed in the fire of the darkened silent room. A gentle hissing sound was heard. This was steam escaping from a hole in the bottle, for the smith had realised that one was necessary to avoid explosions! As the witches brew boiled the spell was removed.

A young girl once sought his help. She had been bewitched by a gipsy for refusing to give her beer belonging to some farm labourers. The poor girl was cursed, became ill, ran on all fours, barked like a dog and meowed like a cat.

The iron bottle was produced and filled with the unpleasant concoction. It was placed on the fire and as the brew boiled footsteps were heard outside the house, followed by a furious knocking on the door and agonised pleas of "For God's sake, stop, you're killing me." At that moment the bottle exploded and the sound of footsteps became fainter and fainter as the tortured female fled into the distance. The following day the body of the gipsy was found, horribly burned, a few miles away.

That Cunning Murrell had genuine powers of healing

cannot be denied, but he did wrap up simple remedies in mumbojumbo to impress his clients. It was not enough to prescribe a simple herbal laxative. An incantation was uttered to bemuse the gullible patient. It is reported that the herbal remedies were not always immediately efficacious, but Murrell countered any complaints by saying that the witch who had cast the spell was a powerful one. Another donation of half-a-crown worked wonders!

Rumours and myths accumulated around him and he did much to encourage them. If called away to a distant farm to cure murrain in cattle, he preferred to travel by night, he arrived mysteriously at dawn and left at dusk, and never bothered to deny that a flying hurdle was his normal mode of transport.

Even Cunning Men had to die but Murrell's exit was in keeping with his life. He consulted his astrological charts and forecast December 16th 1860, as the day of his death. A local curate tried to administer the last rites but the poor man fled in disgust or fear — we are not told which — when the dying man shouted "I am the Devil's master." He returned to that master on the date forecast and was buried in an unmarked grave in Hadleigh churchyard.

Like all witches he hoped that one of his numerous progeny would inherit his powers, but alas! they were not of his ilk. His son Buck made a start. At least he could cure warts and he even tried the iron bottle routine — with disastrous results — the house blew up! He returned to the cure of warts.

After the death of Murrell rumours concerning his magical powers multiplied and stories were circulated about his death. One rival claimed that he had caused the death of Murrell in revenge because the Cunning

Man had bewitched his monkey. Some of the monkey's hair was placed in a bottle together with some of its nail clippings, then the bottle was placed on the fire. There was a loud knocking on the door, which was ignored. The bottle exploded, the knocking ceased and the footsteps died away. Next day Cunning Murrell was found dead.

A well-known local rival of Murrell was Mrs. Eves who lived in a cottage near the "Wagon and Horses", Hadleigh. She was feared as much in death as in life and nobody would volunteer to enter her cottage to lay her out and bury her. Eventually two women from the village overcame their fears and behaved like true neighbours. They had just completed their task when a man entered the dwelling and announced himself as the dead woman's son. His tale was astonishing. He had been working in a field some distance from Hadleigh when the ghost of his mother appeared to him, hence his return home. He was a frightened man and insisted that he did not want to inherit his mother's power. He opened a drawer, took out a box that contained a live creature and threw it on the fire. A frightful human scream scared the neighbours, but as the box and its contents turned to ashes the screams died away. Before the poor women fled from the cottage they noticed that the man's appearance had changed. He looked happy and remarked, "I am free at last."

Sailors are supposed, by tradition, to be superstitious so the sight of old Mother Moore on the river front at Leigh-on-Sea during the fifties of the last century must have struck terror into them. From all accounts she had a frightful appearance — dirty, gaunt and ugly. As the sailors boarded their ships she extended her claw-like hand and screamed, "Buy a fair wind, buy a fair wind."

Old Salts never argued with her, feeling that a few pence was cheap insurance. One day a strange captain refused to throw her a coin and he even had the temerity to laugh at her as he walked along the quay to his ship. He gave orders to cast off and, they sailed into the main stream. Suddenly, the wind dropped and the sails flapped limp. Dark clouds blotted out the sun, turning day into night. Enormous claps of thunder shook the ship, lightning flashed through the rigging as rain deluged the decks in frightening torrents. Even the tough sailors became alarmed at the terror. "This is witches' work," they all shouted. The skipper seemed convinced. He seized an axe, rushed to the bows and as he shouted above the storm, "I'll kill the witch" he struck the prow of the ship three times with all his might.

The storm ceased as suddenly as it had begun. The sun broke through and a fresh wind filled the sails.

When, sometime later, the ship returned to Leigh, the body of Old Mother Moore lay sprawled on the quayside, dead. On her head were three mysterious gashes!

About this time there lived in Canewdon a wise-man named George Pickingill. He is still recalled by some of the older folk of the parish. They remember a tall, gaunt figure and how a mere glance from him put fear into their young hearts. They never lingered as they passed his cottage, but sometimes when they could summon enough courage to look quickly inside they had the feeling that the sparse furniture actually danced. Nobody ever went inside the cottage. Visitors were strictly unwelcome. George was credited with remarkable powers. He had only to whistle and the nine witches of Canewdon would appear immediately at their doors. He was reputed to be truly magical. While he sat in the shade, his non-union imps would mow a field in half an hour flat. He could bewitch machines and this power was inversely proportionate to his thirst. His threat could be bought off with a pint of beer. The picture of a drunken witch conjures up alarming possibilities, so it is perhaps fortunate that George is the only one recorded in Essex, as far as I know. Injuries vanished at his touch and lost property was recovered with equal speed and facility.

When he died, nobody moaned his going. There was a sense of relief in Canewdon, for he was much feared. His life was strange and even his burial had a touch of the bizarre. As the hearse approached the churchyard the horse bolted from the shafts and fled far into the open country.

CHAPTER VIII

Into Witch Country

Cunning Murrell prophesied: "There will be witches in Leigh for a hundred years, and three in Hadleigh and nine in Canewdon." All three villages have a long tradition of witchcraft, but it is Canewdon which, for some mysterious reason had the reputation of being the centre of witchcraft of the county. On July 25th, 1580, "Rose Pye of Canneydon, spinster, on 30th June at Canneydon, bewitched Joan Snow of Canneydon, aged 1 year, daughter of Richard Snow of Canneydon, who languished until 20th August following, when she died at Canneydon."

From that day so long ago to the present, the tradition still persists. The village has changed a great deal through the centuries. The houses that cluster on the hilltop around the ancient church are very modern and the villagers are no longer superstitious peasants like Richard Snow but the belief is still current that witches still exist in Canewdon and that one dies whenever a stone falls from the church tower to be replaced immediately by another.

Eric Maples, who has done so much research into Essex witchcraft, has discovered that local cyclists are still reluctant to ride into the village because of a common belief that their wheels will seize up. This is interesting since it illustrates how traditions persist even when the origin is forgotten. It seems that Canewdon witches were allergic to wheeled traffic, and they did their anti-pollution bit by casting a severe glance in the direction of the offending vehicle and thus bringing it to a sudden halt. We noted that wise-man Pickingill has this power. Maples wondered if some mental confusion had led to the belief that mechanical vehicles could be stopped by witches. In his fascinating study of the horse-cult, Ewart Evans uncovers the age-old mystery of how certain men had the power to stop or start horses at will. Did the ignorant countryman transfer this genuine power from horses to machines? It seems a reasonable explanation.

Frequently village blacksmiths were credited with this ability over vehicles and over horses. But it was not horses that troubled one of the smiths who lived near Canewdon, but white mice. When he was hale and hearty they served him faithfully but as he lay on his deathbed suffering from severe pains, they would not let him die until he had found a successor who would then become their master. His wife refused point blank, but his daughter, moved to compassion by the sight of her suffering father, agreed to accept the familiars into her care. This settled, the old man died peacefully.

The tower of Canewdon church dominates the countryside. It is believed that the massive structure was built by Henry V as a thank offering for his success at Agincourt. It bestrides the hill, from where, four centuries before, Canute and his troops, had gazed westwards toward Ashingdon where Edmund Ironside and his English soldiers were encamped. The historic battle that placed a Dane on the throne of England was probably fought where today Scaldhurst Farm stands, in blissful peace.

From the top of the tower the extensive view embraces a great part of the Essex witch country. To the north the River Crouch gleams silver and inviting on a summer's day, but at times it can be forbidding and angry as it was that night when a witch tried to cross it with her stolen bell. She was one of the notorious Hart family and why she had run off with the bell from her own village church at Latchingdon has never been satisfactorily explained. She was ill-equipped for the enterprise — a tub for a boat and feathers for oars, possibly the worst combination to navigate the treacherous Crouch. Inevitably, the bell finished up stuck fast in the river mud, where it remains to this day. It is said that sometimes, when the night is pitch-black and the savage wind from the North Sea whips the water into a fury, the eerie sound of muffled bells can be heard, and some imaginative people have even claimed to have seen mysterious shapes, for all the world like witches, assemble on the river bank summoned by the call of the bell.

To the east of the church Wallasea Island spreads out flat and low towards the River Roach. In winter when biting winds sweep in from the east and the rain shoots down in icy spears only witches and devils would feel at home there. It comes as no surprise therefore, that the Devil did have a house in this very place. Hurling a beam into the air, he commanded his workmen to erect a house wherever it fell and there it stood until 1953. Old Mother Redcap once lived there but it was one of her earth-bound familiars which gave the place a notoriety. It lived in one of the upstairs rooms and its presence reduced the temperature of the air to that of a deep freeze so that anyone brave enough to venture into it was immediately chilled to the bone and overcome by fear. The coldness was accompanied by a fierce, fluttering of wings. Only one person claims to have seen anything. Returning home late one night he heard his name called but at first saw nothing, then felt a great urge to commit suicide and as he was throwing the rope over a beam he was startled to see a black, ape-like creature with glaring red eyes. His desire to commit suicide passed quickly. He ran home in record time; there is no record that he signed the pledge after the encounter.

Witch Hart of Latchingdon — the one who stole the bell — came of a long line of witches. In the last chapter, John Harriot's description of the "swimming" of the two Harts suspected of causing disease in cattle, is quoted. The last of the line was still living in the early nineteenth century and she too, had the power to bewitch animals. She could also cause disease in crops and like some great Shaman could influence the weather, although being a witch, storms appealed to her most. She was somewhat "kinky" in her choice of abodes, having a predilection for greasy wheel hubs. When she decided to take residence it was not her intention to do the wheel a good turn — quite the reverse. Displacing her was not easy, but she was human enough to respond to a good whipping. A few sturdy lashes and she dropped out covered in blood and mumbling unladylike remarks under her breath.

When dying, she, like all good witches, wanted to pass on her powers and her familiars to a near relative. Unfortunately, her son showed no interest in such an inheritance and did his best to avoid contact with her. However, one day he had to ride past her cottage which stood near Deadaway Bridge. Imagine his terror when a horde of white mice left the cottage and headed at top speed in his direction. The horse did not like the sight either, and drew on a reserve of speed which it must have kept for just such an occasion. The mice were easily outpaced — and the hereditary powers of Mother Hart were broken.

Two people of the same village also possessed unusual powers although to a much lesser degree. They were ex-constable Buzzy and his bosom friend, known to one and all by the unflattering nickname, Silly Billy. Both had the ability which we have noticed before of being able to stop and start machinery by simply glancing in the direction of the contraption. The tale is told that on one occasion they noticed that the driver of a steam tractor had succumbed to the common practice of extending his mid-day break, so they cast their combined glances at the tractor which immediately started to crawl along. The driver, amazed and frightened, gulped down his final morsels then galloped down the lane in pursuit of the disappearing machine.

The road from Latchingdon to Tillingham is of the Chesterton type. It rolls drunkenly across the countryside, so it is no wonder that witches found it quicker by broom, provided the local man and wife witch-team was not up to its tricks again of interfering with the weather! Mr. and Mrs. Bird possessed this power but sometimes there seemed to be something lacking in their formula. On one occasion, for instance, they had conjured up a truly magnificent storm but the lightning got out of control, striking the witch on the arm and the man in the leg. Ever afterwards, superstitious peasants found no difficulty in recognising the witch in the village. Mr. Bird had a club foot and his wife a withered arm.

A rose by any other name . . . said Shakespeare. Even

when witchcraft was officially dead its practice in the country under various guises, continued. Superstitious villagers recognised it and in sudden outbursts gave vent to their primitive fears. In Essex one of the saddest and cruellest incidents took place in Sible Hedingham in 1863.

A tall, gaunt man, of forbidding experience lived in a mud hut outside the village. Since he seldom spoke, and never took anybody into his confidence, he was a man of mystery. His place of birth, his occupation, even his name were unknown. It was thought that he was French but since his tongue had been cut out even this was not certain. His habit of wearing two or three hats and two or three coats was not a characteristic to inspire confidence. And the several little dogs that followed him around looked all the world like witches' imps. Because he lacked speech he was nicknamed Dummy.

North of Sible Hedingham is Ridgewell, quite near the Suffolk border. One night a knock brought Emma Smith to the door of her cottage. The strange-looking man standing before her sent a chill down her spine. She was made to understand by sign language and grunts that he wanted a lodging for the night. Not surprisingly she said no.

Shortly afterwards she fell sick and her peasant mind recalled the odd figure of a few days before and the way in which he had mumbled as he slouched away from her cottage. Evidently he had cast a spell over her. She argued that if he would now accept her hospitality the spell would be removed and she would recover. She located him in the "Swan" inn, Sible Hedingham.

Not unnaturally, Dummy refused her invitation. The outcast was suspicious and strongly resisted her pleas. Her persistence led to a violent quarrel in which bystanders joined, chiefly on the side of Emma Smith.

All the latent anger of the villagers came to the surface fanned into flame by the local bully, Samuel Stammers.

When Dummy left the "Swan" the mob followed him as he made his way back to his hovel. As he neared the river, Emma Smith seized him by his coat and pushed him into the water. He tried to get out on the opposite bank but she and Stammers ran across the bridge and pushed him in again. The next time he managed to climb onto the bank but he was immediately grabbed and thrown into deeper water. The crowd, many of whom had tagged along just for the fun of it, was now becoming rather frightened by their own violence and realised that what they were abetting was no longer a joke, so they quickly disappeared and allowed the wretched hermit to crawl to the shelter of his mud hut. He never did recover from his awful ordeal. Some villagers had him removed to the comparative comfort of the work-house where, a month later, he died.

Seventeen years later the last case of "swimming" in the whole of England took place in Dunmow. Two insomniac brothers called Brewster claimed that the cause of their sleepless nights was Susan Sharpe. They had seen her shadow quite clearly and recognisably on their bedroom wall. The witch of a woman was accused of causing their bed to rock violently like a "swinging boat". After consulting a cunning man they had acted on his advice by trying to "persuade" her to submit to the swimming test. She strongly objected to the outrageous suggestion and quite rightly reported the matter in the proper quarters. She explained that the brothers had pestered her for over twenty years. They had made her life a misery. She had never complained before, but this "swimming" was just too much. The Brewsters were bound over. The year was 1880.

CHAPTER IX

Witch Remedies in Essex

Many and varied were the spells cast by witches. There seems to have been nothing, animate or inanimate, free from their occult powers. Humans, though, were the main victims. The "languishing" into which so many of them lapsed could have been mental in origin, as suggested by that old sceptic, Scot. Witchdoctors, palmists, clairvoyants, not to mention the numerous Madame Zaras that add variety and colour to our fairs and fêtes, employ this well-known principle.

If people could be bewitched into illness, they could also be "unwitched". An application of a poultice made from herbs, or goose grease or some other revolting concoction to the affected part, or the drinking of an elixir the taste of which was sometimes more unbearable than the ailment, would cure the complaint, but how much more effective if the remedies were administered in a darkened room hanging with herbs, with a skull on the table and maybe a black cat or ferret lurking furtively in the corners, and the witch or cunning-man mumbling strange-sounding incantations. I have an early memory of such an experience. Accidentally, scalding water had been poured over my bare knees. My sister reacted instantly and fetched the neighbourhood witch. She saw the damage and applied her herbal balm. The pain vanished at once and next day there was not a blister or a red mark to be seen. But what lingers still in my mind is the soothing, lilting Welsh incantation murmured as the white witch applied the ointment.

You will recall that when Buck Murrell's excursion into the more esoteric realms of witchcraft proved so disastrous, he returned to the charming of warts. We do not know which method he employed. Perhaps he allowed snails to crawl over the growth or perhaps he practised a remedy given me recently by an old Burnham farmer. He swore that if you took a branch from the elder tree and cut a notch in it for every wart defiling your skin, then before the stick withered the warts would disappear.

Cures for other ailments were equally strange in the Essex witch country. The "hair of the dog" is an established cure for a hangover, but did you know that a dog's hair (an actual one this time) placed between two slices of bread and then eaten would cure whooping cough? Or that deafness could be cured if a fresh ivy leaf were placed in the ear every morning? In his travels throughout England, Daniel Defoe made great play of the ague and similar complaints that affected the marsh dwellers of Essex, but he did not suggest a remedy. The Essex cure was simple, if a trifle unusual. Take a spoonful of gunpowder and exercise immediately afterwards. No reports of its efficacy have reached our ears.

Burrows, the well known Essex historian, uncovered other remedies when researching witch-lore in the Rochford Hundred. Rheumatism and ague were thought to attack from the ground upwards so, like the old navvy who wore "yorks" just below the knee to keep the dust out of his eyes — so it is said — sufferers from the two marsh complaints were advised by the wise-man to wear a sealskin garter against rheumatism and a bag of camphor tied in the same place, against cramp. A snakeskin, if worn inside the hat, was also efficacious in curing headaches. Equally illogical was another cure for whooping cough. First catch your flounder then dip a lump of sugar in its blood. Allow to dissolve in mouth. Repeat the process until cough disappears. A sweeter cure is that for bee stings — apply honey to the affected part. The remedy for sore eyes is positively poetic — bathe the eyes with the first raindrops to fall on the first day of June.

It seemed that these remedies which originated in the mind of the witch, or cunning man, became common property, a part of country lore, and could be used by anybody without witchcraft knowledge. More serious complaints demanded the intervention of a witch. Nelly Button of Hockley who lived in the sixties of the last century, had among other powers, the ability to paralyse her enemies with her evil eye. No herbal mixture was effective in removing the spell — only a magic murmur in the ear of the victim was of any avail.

Fire and its near neighbour, a red hot poker, were anathema to witches and their spells. When the layman resorted to such remedies the results were sometimes extremely painful if not disastrous. A farmer in Billericay thrust a red hot poker down the throat of his sick colt in an endeavour to banish the spell... The poor creature never suffered from the murrain after the treatment. It died.

Bewitched milk could also be cured with the red hot poker treatment. The method was doubly effective since it also burned the witch at the same time. This occurred, for instance, when Diddy Horn cast a spell on the butter-making of a local farmer. He guessed what had happened when the milk would not turn, so he thrust the red hot poker into the churn. Not only was the spell broken but Diddy Horn was severely burnt. She was last seen leaving the village at top speed, never to return.

In the records of Essex witchcraft I have discovered only one case of bewitched plants. It occurred in Dunmow as recently as 1920. A horticulturist of that town was remarkedly successful at all the shows held in the neighbourhood. His rivals noticed that shortly before a show only their exhibits were attacked by birds. Since he was a fortune-teller by profession, it was assumed that witchcraft and not fertiliser was the basis of his usual success.

Cases where witchcraft was turned to useful domestic purposes are surprisingly rare. Old man Pickingill used his imps at harvest time but female witches seemed to be very unimaginative and unenterprising. A modern witch of my acquaintance was one of the dirtiest persons imaginable, both in her person and home — and, being without humour, saw nothing strange in calling herself a white witch! Why she never used her powers to keep her house clean is difficult to fathom. Perhaps it was for the same reason as Margaret Wyseman.

Margaret was accused by Timothy Wardell of Maldon of being a witch. This she denied and since Timothy was unable to prove his allegation, she was released and he was bound over to keep the peace. This he did, but other villagers did not. Tongues wagged and Margaret was brought once again before the magistrate in June 1591 and was again accused of practising witchcraft. She claimed that she was innocent of the charges and found support in an unsuspected quarter. Her previous enemy, Timothy Wardell maintained that "he never reported that he sawe the broome sweepe the house, alone, without hands, nor had any cause to saye." This testimony secured Margaret's release, but failed to subdue entirely an envious interest in the case of the automated broom.

CHAPTER X

Witchcraft Today

Witchcraft is not dead. On the contrary it is very much alive. The last twenty years have seen a great revival of interest in the cult. Books on the subject proliferate. Its causes and development have been analysed by the social anthropologist; its practice described by men like the late Gerald Gardiner, and the darker side dramatised by writers like Dennis Wheatley.

Television, too, has played its part in the revival. From time to time the late viewer is regaled with film of members of well fed covens, for all the world like refugees from a better class golf club, gambolling blithely but self-consciously in the nude in the grassy glades of woods deep in the Surrey stockbroker belt. Occasionally, excursions into Essex witch country are taken.

There is much confusion in the popular mind concerning present-day witchcraft. This is not surprising when the more sensational press makes no distinction between its various forms. Broadly speaking, the ancient categories still persist — simple herbal healing, black witchcraft and white witchcraft.

We have observed that during the two centuries of the great purges, even an innocent villager who possessed the gift of healing by means of herbs and autosuggestion was regarded as a witch. With the advance of medicine the awe with which such a person was treated became somewhat dimmed, but village healers never passed into oblivion. Strangely enough there has been a revival of interest in their remedies. It is not unusual for intelligent people to shun drugs concocted in the laboratory and seek solace and even cure in more ancient and tried recipes derived from natural, growing plants.

Black witchcraft is not practised to any great extent in this country. Certainly not in Essex. Readers of the works of Aleister Crowley, self-styled Beast 999 and the sensational fiction of Dennis Wheatley, will know that the cult is quite alien to the English tradition and one not to be encouraged or practised. From time to time newspapers report the desecration of gravestones or the removal of sacred objects from a church and devotees of the Black Arts are held responsible. This could be true. Until quite recently there was a life-sized cat carved out of stone to be seen in Canewdon church. The sculptor had succeeded in turning a domestic pet into a fierce and frightening creature, fit companion for a witch. The evil appearance of the beast and the fact that it was in Canewdon, might explain why it was stolen. Is it now being used in some Black Witchcraft ceremony?

The present vicar thinks that originally the cat was a gargoyle on some west country church. This is interesting since gargoyles were placed on the north parapet of churches in order to scare away evil spirits and witches. The north side of the churchyard was also the place where witches were buried.

White witchcraft receives less publicity than the black variety. White covens do not complain of this treatment, in fact they welcome it. They never advertise their activities and never canvass for new members. They believe that those rare people who possess exceptional psychic powers, will gravitate naturally to others of similar beliefs.

Because of this cultivated reticence, the non-witch finds it difficult to locate members of the Old Religion and even when successful the true witch is always reluctant to discuss her beliefs and practices. Books are not lacking to fill the gap but, as with Freemasonry, a literary account of the craft is but a pale reflection of the truth. The mystique cannot be described, it can only be experienced. Only by taking part in the ceremonial ritual can a true and full understanding be obtained.

And yet in this chapter, I have boldly indicated certain features of witchcraft. Although brief, they have been pronounced accurate by one who should know.

White witches maintain that theirs is the Old Religion, predating Christianity. For evidence they cite palaeolithic cave drawings of shamans, the nature of their secret ritual and the pantheism in which they believe. It is matriarchal, with a High Priestess who has the power and authority to appoint a High Priest. Devotees worship a God and a Goddess, but they explain that these deities are mere symbols, a means of concentrating the minute mind of man on a concept at once infinite and inconceivable.

At their meetings, witches worship in the nude, not to take part in sexual orgies, as is generally supposed, but in the belief that only in this state, untrammelled by the unnatural restrictions of clothes, can they be in harmony with Nature and thus absorb more easily a fraction of the Power of the all-pervading Spirit which is Life itself.

Fertility rites do still play an important part in the

Sabbats, as they have since the dawn of history, but the meaning has undergone change in order to adjust to the modern world. Originally, the practice was a magical means of increasing the yield of the crops or the success of the hunt.

Nowadays, since so many people are strangers to the fields and woods and the needs of the inner man can so easily be obtained from the corner shop or the ubiquitous supermarket, fertility rites have lost their primitive significance. But, argue the witches, those who take part in these magic rites today are rewarded. The primitive urges of Man, his deepest emotions, are awakened to pervade the whole body, mind and spirit. Life is enriched beyond measure. Life is worth living.

Printed by Maund & Irvine Ltd., Tring, Herts.